HAPPY NEW YEAR!

BY BECKY GOLD
ILLUSTRATED BY NICON CARRERA

Scott Foresman
is an imprint of

Glenview, Illinois • Boston, Massachusetts • Chandler, Arizona •
Upper Saddle River, New Jersey

Photographs

Every effort has been made to secure permission and provide appropriate credit for photographic material. The publisher deeply regrets any omission and pledges to correct errors called to its attention in subsequent editions.

Unless otherwise acknowledged, all photographs are the property of Pearson Education, Inc.

20 STR/AFP/Getty Images.

ISBN 13: 978-0-328-51344-4
ISBN 10:   0-328-51344-X

11 12 13 14   V010   18 17 16 15 14

Jackson Kramer watched excitedly as fluffy, white flakes floated down outside his window. Finally, the first snow of the year—and just in time for winter vacation!

"I hope we can build a snow fort," Jackson told his cat, Monster, who purred loudly.

Suddenly, his younger sister Sonia bounced into the room. "Jackson!" she shouted. "There's a moving van midway down the street!"

Jackson craned his neck to see. A big box truck with the words "TLC Movers" was parked in front of the brick house.

Jackson flew downstairs, with Sonia on his heels.

"We'll be right back," Jackson called to their father, pulling on his jacket.

"What's the hurry?" Mr. Kramer asked from the kitchen.

"We're going to see the new neighbors!" Sonia said. She began to put her jacket on too.

They raced outside just as a blue car pulled into the nearby driveway and stopped in the middle. A man and woman got out.

"There's a kid in the back seat," Sonia whispered. "Oh, now I see two kids!"

Jackson saw movement in the back seat too.

A boy who looked about Jackson's age emerged from the car. An older girl followed. The parents began to walk up the path but the boy hung back, walking slowly. Jackson wondered if he was homesick.

"Hi," Jackson said.

The boy looked up, startled.

"My name's Jackson Kramer," he said. "What's yours?"

"Jun Yang."

The boy's voice was so quiet that Jackson had to bend forward to hear him.

"Where are you from?" Jackson asked.

"Hong Kong, China," Jun said.

Jun introduced Jackson and Sonia to his family.

"It is very nice to meet you," said Mrs. Yang, smiling.

"Same here," Jackson said. Suddenly Jackson felt shy.

"See you later," he said as he began to lead Sonia back toward home.

Later that afternoon, Mrs. Kramer said, "We should welcome the Yangs to our neighborhood. Let's make a welcome basket for them with treats and some useful things, like a town map."

Sonia said, "Hmmm. I have an idea. Let's also invite them to First Night!"

Every New Year's Eve, Jackson's town had a First Night festival. Last year, they'd gone to the high school, where there were classes and performances all night long. Jackson and his sister had learned how to juggle and had listened to a jazz band perform. Later, neighbors and friends had come by to watch the fireworks.

"Sonia," said Mr. Kramer, "that's a terrific idea."

"I think so too," Mrs. Kramer agreed. "First Night is so much fun."

The next morning, Jackson woke to find two feet of snow on the ground.

After breakfast, the Kramer family walked to Jun's house. They introduced themselves, and Mrs. Yang invited them in to meet the family. Then Mrs. Kramer invited the Yangs to celebrate First Night with them. The Yangs happily agreed.

"Jun, do you want to play?" Jackson asked, bored with the grown-ups' conversation.

The boys went to the backyard to build a snow fort.

"How do you celebrate the New Year?" Jackson asked.

Jun said, "We usually eat delicious foods, watch a dragon parade, and give each other gifts. We also stay up late, just like you do. This year, in the Chinese calendar, New Year's comes a few weeks from now. And so we'll celebrate then."

"Each year is named for a different animal," Jun continued. "The new year that's coming up is the year of the ox. People born in that year are said to be like that animal. Let's say someone was born in 2000, which is the year of the dragon. People say that any person born a dragon is very enthusiastic. There's even a legend that says dragons are the stars of the universe."

"Wow!" said Jackson.

Just as Jackson and Jun finished their fort, Jackson's parents said it was time to go home. During the walk home, Jackson realized there was so much more he wanted to know about Jun's culture. He couldn't wait to see him again and learn more about it.

Jackson couldn't wait to take Jun to First Night. Now, he'd be able to show Jun how Americans celebrate New Year's.

In the meantime, he'd gone to the library and checked out some books on China. Ever since learning about Chinese New Year, he wanted to know everything about China.

On December 31, Jackson's family spent the day cleaning the house, cooking, and baking. They expected a crowd of people to come over after the celebration.

When it got dark, the Jacksons bundled up and made their way to Jun's house. Then, the two families walked into town.

"Wow!" Jun said, pushing open the door of the gymnasium. There were people everywhere. It was noisy as well. In one corner, kids were making large puppets out of papier-mâché.

"I have an idea," Jun said, pointing at the puppets. "Let's make a dragon! Then we can parade it for the New Year."

"You mean tonight?" Jackson asked.

"No, on *Chinese* New Year!"

The boys shaped the papier-mâché head as Sonia looked on. Then, the three of them went to the clown room to watch clowns perform and then to listen to a band play old-time music while they waited for the dragon's head to dry. Everyone was dancing and eating and having a great time! Once the dragon was dry, Jun, Jackson, and Sonia returned to the gym to paint the dragon's head and add a long tail. Sonia was especially good at painting, so the boys let her help with that part.

The hours passed quickly. Soon it was time to go home. Carefully, Jun and Jackson lifted up the dragon and carried it with them. They tried to hide it with their coats as best they could. They wanted it to be a surprise. The families looked like a small parade as they headed back to Jackson's house.

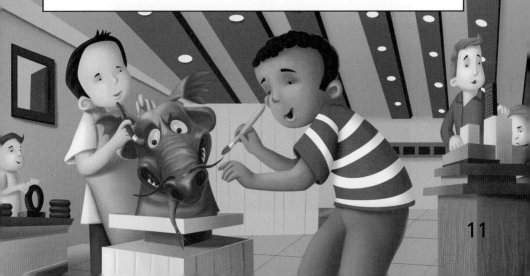

The house quickly filled with people. Jackson introduced his friends to Jun, who seemed glad to meet them. Sonia was so tired that she fell asleep right away on the couch.

Everyone talked, laughed, and filled their plates with food.

"Breakfast at night," Jun told Jackson. "I like this idea!"

A while later, Jackson's father shouted, "It's almost midnight! The fireworks are about to go off!"

Hurriedly they bundled up and went outside to watch a beautiful and noisy display in the sky over town.

The next morning, Jackson helped his parents clean up the living room.

"First Night was a big success," Mrs. Kramer said.

"Do you think Jun's family enjoyed themselves?" asked Mr. Kramer.

Jackson nodded.

"What was *your* favorite part?"

Jackson scratched his cheek. "Sharing our tradition with Jun."

"Oh, then you'll be happy to know," said his mother, "that Mrs. Yang invited us to their Chinese New Year celebration later this month."

Jackson couldn't wait. That would be the perfect time to reveal their dragon!

Two days before Chinese New Year, Jun asked Jackson if he'd like to come over.

Jun's house looked different. There was a red scroll on the front door. In the kitchen, there was a picture of a jolly fat man, with sweets and other foods on a shelf below him.

"Who's that?" Jackson asked.

"That's Zao Jun, the kitchen god. He watches over our home every day, making sure we're being good all year long."

"He also makes sure we appreciate all the good things we have to eat," Mrs. Yang added. "Come on, Jackson. Let's cook, and I'll tell you Zao Jun's story."

As Jackson learned to make Chinese dumplings, he watched Jun place food on a shelf below the picture of Zao Jun.

Mrs. Yang said, "Zao Jun watches over us all year long. We put out good things for him to eat so that he will only say sweet things about us."

She smiled. "One year, the people in China were upset because Zao Jun told the heavens bad things about them. The heavens grew angry, and bad things happened to the people—floods, droughts, and destruction. The following year, people had the idea to set out melon candies. The kitchen god stuffed his mouth so full that he couldn't say a thing. Now, we do it each year."

Before Jackson knew it, it was time to go.

"Gung hay fat choy!" Jun said. "That means 'Happy New Year.'"

Jackson hoped he wouldn't mispronounce the Chinese words when he said, "Gung hay fat choy!"

Jun smiled.

When the time finally came to celebrate Chinese New year, Jun met Jackson's family at the door. Jackson carried a big box.

"Gung hay fat choy!" Jackson said, as they entered the Yang's house.

The families sat down to eat. There were long noodles, which represented a long life. There was a delicious, crispy fish and a roasted duck. There were Nin Go, sweet New Year's cakes, and other treats.

Jun and Jackson looked at each other, and grinned. The box Jackson brought in contained a surprise that they had planned.

"In China," Mr. Yang said, "the children also stay up as late as they can on New Year's. The later they stay up, the longer their parents' and grandparents' lives will be." He winked at Jun.

"We're going to stay up all night, aren't we, Jackson?" Jun said.

Jackson nodded, his mouth full of noodles.

"In Hong Kong," Mr. Yang said, "the dragon parade is an important New Year's ceremony. We could see the dragon parade from the windows of our apartment. We'd open the windows, and our whole family would crowd around to watch."

"You wouldn't believe how noisy it was, with all the firecrackers going off!" Jun said.

Jun's sister Shen looked sad. "I think she really misses her grandma," Mrs. Yang said. "They are very close. This is her first Chinese New Year without her grandma. Shen took pictures of your New Year's and sent them back home. I hope that she will be in better spirits and take some pictures tonight too."

"Oh, I bet she will," Jun said, mysteriously. "Jackson, let's bring that box upstairs."

Jun picked up the box and raced upstairs with Jackson right behind him. When they were safely in Jun's room, they opened the box and gently pulled out the dragon head and tail. With Jun inside the head and Jackson holding the tail, they went down the hallway.

Jun knocked on the door to Shen's room. After a moment, Shen opened it. She looked as if she'd been crying again. But when she saw the dragon's head, she smiled.

"Wait," she said and went to her dresser. She came back with her camera.

With a whoop, the boys came running down the stairs. Everyone laughed and clapped and cheered as the boys paraded around the table and through the living room.

"Come on!" Jun shouted. "Join us!"

Still clapping, everyone got up from their seats and followed the dragon.

A few days later, the Yangs took the Kramers to Chinatown in nearby New York City to continue their New Year's celebration. Jackson was amazed by the crowds, the colors, and the noise of the festival. He also wasn't used to a New Year's celebration that lasted 15 days!

Afterward, they went to a restaurant. The diners all wished one another a "Happy New Year" in Chinese.

Mr. Yang said, "Having such nice friends makes life sweet."

"And having two New Year's celebrations is twice as sweet!" Sonia said.

Everyone laughed because they knew what Sonia had said was true.

New Year's Celebrations Around the World

The New Year is celebrated in different ways all over the world. In Australia, on January first, many people take a picnic to the beach or go to a rodeo. In Egypt, children are given special sweets. Boys get a sweet molded in the shape of a boy on horseback, and girls get a sweet molded in the shape of a girl wearing a dress. In South Africa, people ring church bells and fire guns to celebrate. In Russia, Grandfather Frost, who looks a lot like Santa Claus, visits children with a big bag of gifts!